The Book of
Kids Songs
A Holler-Along Handbook

by Nancy Cassidy
illustrated by Jim M'Guinness
music produced by Ken Whiteley

KLUTZ PRESS, PALO ALTO, CALIFORNIA

Design, Art Direction, Production, and Hand Lettering:
MaryEllen Podgorski and Suzanne Gooding

Illustrations: Jim M'Guinness

Music Production and Direction: Ken Whiteley

Music Transcription: Barbara Allen Roberts

Additional Copies

KIDSSONGS is actually just the first book + cassette package in the KIDSSONGS series. For information about the other members of the series, please refer to the order form on the back of the card inserted into the cassette case.

Replacement copies of the book itself (without cassette) are $2.50 + $2.00 handling.

Free Catalogue

For a complete collection of all the Klutz books and products, please send for our free catalogue. The Klutz Flying Apparatus Catalogue, 2121 Staunton Court, Palo Alto, CA 94306. Or you can call us at (415) 424-0739.

4   1

ISBN 0-932592-13-9

Published by Klutz Press,
Palo Alto, California

Song

List

You Gotta Sing

Traditional

You got - ta sing when your spir - it says

sing, You got - ta sing when your spir - it says

sing, When your spir - it says sing you got - ta

sing right a - long, You got - ta

sing when your spir - it says sing.

You gotta shout when your spirit says shout,
You gotta shout when your spirit says shout,
When your spirit says shout you gotta shout right out loud,
You gotta shout when your spirit says shout.

You gotta wiggle when your spirit says wiggle,
You gotta wiggle when your spirit says wiggle,
When your spirit says wiggle, you gotta wiggle like a worm,
You gotta wiggle when your spirit says wiggle.

You gotta shake when your spirit says shake,
You gotta shake when your spirit says shake,
When your spirit says shake, you gotta shake like a snake,
You gotta shake when your spirit says shake.

You gotta dance when your spirit says dance,
You gotta dance when your spirit says dance,
When your spirit says dance you gotta dance right along,
You gotta dance when your spirit says dance.

You gotta sing when your spirit says sing,
You gotta sing when your spirit says sing,
When your spirit says sing, you gotta sing right along,
You gotta sing when your spirit says sing.

Wabash Cannonball

Traditional

From the wide Pa - ci - fic O - cean to the broad At - lan - tic shore, She

climbs the flowery moun - tains o - ver hills and by the shore, Al -

though she's tall and handsome, she's known quite well by all, She's a

reg - u - lar com - bin - a - tion, the Wa - bash Can -non- ball.

Oh Lis - ten to the jin - gle, to the rum - ble and the roar, As she

flies a - long the wood-lands, o-ver hills and by the shore, Hear the

mighty rush of the en - gine, hear the mer-ry ho - bo's squall, As she

rum - bles thru the jun - gles, the Wa - bash Can-non-ball.

Now the eastern states are dandy so the western people say,
From New York to St. Louis, Chicago, by the way,
Through the hills of Minnesota where the rippling waters fall,
No chances to be taken on the Wabash Cannonball.

CHORUS

Day-O

Traditional

Day-o, me say day-o, Day-light come and me

wan-na go home, Day-o, me say day- o,

Day-light come and me wan-na go home, Work all night 'til the

morn-in' come, Day-light come and me wan-na go home,

Stack ba-na-na 'til the morn-in' come, Day-light come and me

wan-na go home, Come mis-ter tal-ly-man, tal-ly me ba-nan-a,

Day-light come and me wan-na go home, Come mis-ter tal-ly-man,

tal-ly me ba-nan-a, Day-light come and me wan-na go home,

CHORUS

A beautiful bunch o' ripe banana,
Daylight come and me wanna go home,
Lift six hand, seven hand, eight hand bunch,
Daylight come and me wanna go home.

> Come mister tallyman, tally me banana,
> Daylight come and me wanna go home,
> Come mister tallyman, tally me banana,
> Daylight come and me wanna go home.

CHORUS

Day-o, me say day-o,
Daylight come and me wanna go home.

11

Ting-A-Lay-O

Traditional

Ting- a- lay- o, run my lit - tle don - key run, Ting-a- lay- o, run my lit - tle don - key run. My don - key hee, my don - key haw, My don- key sleep in a bed of straw, My don- key short, my don - key wide, Don't get too close to his back side.

My donkey walk, my donkey talk,
My donkey eats with a knife and fork,
My donkey eat, my donkey sleep,
My donkey kicks with his two hind feet.

CHORUS

My donkey laugh, my donkey cry,
My donkey loves peanut butter pie,
My donkey laugh, my donkey cry,
My donkey loves peanut butter pie.

CHORUS (twice)

Mister Sun

Traditional

Oh Mis - ter Sun, Sun, Mis - ter Gol - den Sun

Please shine down on me. Oh Mis - ter Sun, Sun,

Mis - ter Gol - den Sun Hid - ing be - hind a tree.

These lit - tle chil - dren are ask - ing you, To

please come out so we can play with you. Oh Mis - ter

Sun, Sun, Mis - ter Gol - den Sun Please shine down on me.

Oh Mister Moon, Moon, bright and silvery moon,
Please shine down on me.
Oh Mister Moon, Moon, bright and silvery moon,
Come from behind that tree.

I like to ramble, I like to roam,
But I like to find myself at home.
When the moon, moon, bright and silvery moon,
Comes shining down on me.

MAKE **S**YOUR OWN poons

Materials: Two metal spoons.

Instructions: Hold the spoons as shown, back to back. The trick is to hold them loosely enough so that they can rattle against one another, but not so loosely that they go flying around the room. Hold your other hand over your knee and tap the spoons between the heel of your hand and your knee.

Father's Old Grey Whiskers

Traditional

I have a dear old dad-dy, For whom I night-ly pray, He

has a set of whis-kers, They're al-ways in the way. They're

al-ways in the way, The cows eat them for hay, They

hide the dirt on Dad-dy's shirt, They're al-ways in the way.

Around the supper table,
We make a happy group,
Until dear father's whiskers,
Get tangled in the soup.

CHORUS

Father had a strong back,
But now it's all caved in,
He stepped upon his whiskers,
And walked up to his chin.

CHORUS

We have a dear old mother,
With him at night she sleeps,
She wakes up in the morning,
Eating shredded wheat.

CHORUS (twice)

Baby Beluga

Raffi and D. Pike

Ba - by Be - lu - ga in the deep blue sea,

Swim so wild and swim so free; Heav-en a-bove and the

sea be-low, And a lit - tle white whale on the go.

Ba - by Be - lu - ga, Ba - by Be -

lu - ga, Is the wa - ter warm,

Is your ma- ma home, With you so hap - py?

Music by Raffi. Words by Raffi and D. Pike © 1980 Homeland Publishing.

Way down yonder where the dolphins play,
Where you dive and splash all day,
Waves roll in and the waves roll out,
See the water squirtin' out of your spout.

Baby Beluga, Baby Beluga,
Sing your little song,
Sing for all your friends,
We like to hear you.

When it's dark, and you're home and fed,
Curl up snug in your water bed,
Moon is shining and the stars are out,
Good night, little whale good night.

Baby Beluga, Baby Beluga,
With tomorrow's sun, another day's begun,
You'll soon be waking.

Baby Beluga in the deep blue sea,
Swim so wild and swim so free;
Heaven above and the sea below,
And a little white whale on the go,
You're just a little white whale on the go.

Willoughby, Wallaby, Woo

Larry Miyata/Dennis Lee

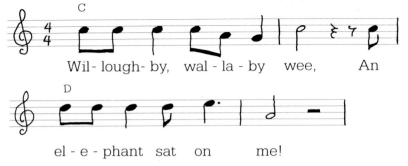

Wil- lough- by, wal - la - by wee, An
el - e - phant sat on me!

Willoughby, wallaby wustin,
An elephant sat on Justin!

Willoughby, wallaby wody,
An elephant sat on Cody!

Willoughby, wallaby wanny,
An elephant sat on Nanny!

Willoughby, wallaby wen,
An elephant sat on Ken!

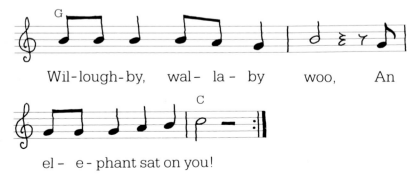

Wil- lough- by, wal - la - by woo, An
el - e - phant sat on you!

Based on "Alligator Pie" a poem by Dennis Lee © 1974 MacMillan Co. of Canada Ltd. Used by permission. Music by Larry Miyata. Adapted lyrics by Raffi © 1976 Homeland Publishing.

Kumbaya

Traditional

Kum- ba- ya, Lord, kum-ba- ya,

Kum-ba- ya, Lord, kum- ba- ya,

Kum- ba- ya, Lord, kum-ba- ya,

Oh   Lord,   kum-ba- ya.

Someone's singing Lord, kum-ba-ya,
Someone's singing Lord, kum-ba-ya,
Someone's singing Lord, kum-ba-ya,
Oh Lord, kum-ba-ya.

Someone's dancing Lord, kum-ba-ya,
Someone's dancing Lord, kum-ba-ya,
Someone's dancing Lord, kum-ba-ya,
Oh Lord, kum-ba-ya.

Someone's crying Lord, kum-ba-ya,
Someone's crying Lord, kum-ba-ya,
Someone's crying Lord, kum-ba-ya,
Oh Lord, kum-ba-ya.

Come by here my Lord, kum-ba-ya,
Come by here my Lord, kum-ba-ya,
Come by here my Lord, kum-ba-ya,
Oh Lord, kum-ba-ya.

Sand Blocks

Materials: Two hand-sized blocks of wood, glue, two pieces of sandpaper.

Instructions: Glue or staple the sandpaper to one side of the two pieces of wood. Then rub the two blocks together.

Shake My Sillies Out

Raffi, Bert and Bonnie Simpson

Got - ta shake, shake, shake my sil - lies out,

Shake, shake, shake my sil - lies out, Shake, shake,

shake my sil - lies out, And wig - gle my wag - gles a - way.

Gotta clap, clap, clap my crazies out,
Clap, clap, clap my crazies out,
Clap, clap, clap my crazies out,
And wiggle my waggles away.

Gotta jump, jump, jump my jiggles out,
Jump, jump, jump my jiggles out,
Jump, jump, jump my jiggles out,
And wiggle my waggles away.

Gotta yawn, yawn, yawn my sleepies out,
Yawn, yawn, yawn my sleepies out,
Yawn, yawn, yawn my sleepies out,
And wiggle my waggles away.

Gotta stretch, stretch, stretch my stretchies out,
Stretch, stretch, stretch my stretchies out,
Stretch, stretch, stretch my stretchies out,
And wiggle my waggles away.

Gotta shake, shake, shake my sillies out,
Shake, shake, shake my sillies out,
Shake, shake, shake my sillies out,
And wiggle my waggles away.

Music by Raffi. Words by Raffi, B. & B. Simpson © 1977 Homeland Publishing.

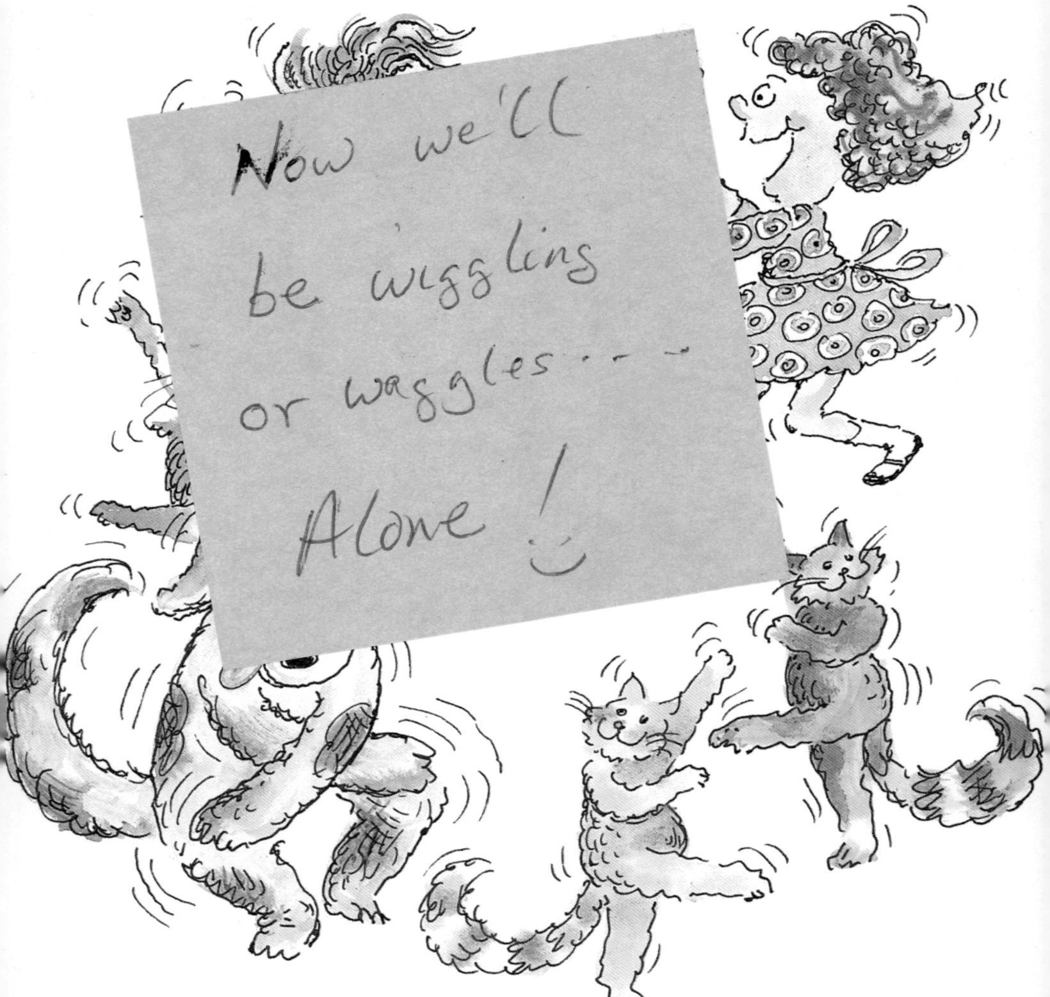
Now we'll
be wiggling
or waggles . . .
Alone!

Brush Your Teeth

Traditional

When you wake up in the morn-ing and it's quar-ter to one, — And you want to have a lit-tle fun, You brush your teeth, ch, ch, ch, ch, ch, ch, ch, ch, ch, — You brush your teeth, ch, ch, ch, ch, ch, ch, ch, ch, ch.

When you wake up in the morning and it's quarter to two,
And you don't know what to do,
You brush your teeth, ch, ch, ch, ch, ch, ch, ch, ch,
You brush your teeth, ch, ch, ch, ch, ch, ch, ch, ch.

When you wake up in the morning and it's quarter to three,
You've got a great big smile for me,
You brush your teeth, ch, ch, ch, ch, ch, ch, ch, ch,
You brush your teeth, ch, ch, ch, ch, ch, ch, ch, ch.

When you wake up in the morning and it's quarter to four,
You hear a great big knock on the door,
You brush your teeth, ch, ch, ch, ch, ch, ch, ch, ch,
You brush your teeth, ch, ch, ch, ch, ch, ch, ch, ch.

When you wake up in the morning and it's quarter to five,
You're so happy to be alive,
You brush your teeth, ch, ch, ch, ch, ch, ch, ch, ch,
You brush your teeth, ch, ch, ch, ch, ch, ch, ch, ch.

Down by the Bay

Traditional

Down by the bay, where the wa-ter-mel-ons grow, Back to my home, I dare not go, For if I do, my moth-er will say... Did you ev- er see a goose, kiss - ing a moose, Down by the bay? Down by the bay?

Down by the bay, where the watermelons grow,
Back to my home, I dare not go,
For if I do, my mother will say...
Did you ever see a whale, with a polka dot tail,
Down by the bay?

28

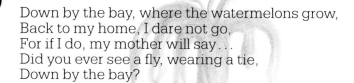

Down by the bay, where the watermelons grow,
Back to my home, I dare not go,
For if I do, my mother will say...
Did you ever see a fly, wearing a tie,
Down by the bay?

Down by the bay, where the watermelons grow,
Back to my home, I dare not go,
For if I do, my mother will say...
Did you ever see a bear, combing his hair,
Down by the bay?

Down by the bay, where the watermelons grow,
Back to my home, I dare not go,
For if I do, my mother will say...
Did you ever see llamas, eating their pajamas,
Down by the bay?

Down by the bay, where the watermelons grow,
Back to my home, I dare not go,
For if I do, my mother will say...
Did you ever see an octupus, dancing with a platypus,
Down by the bay?

Down by the bay, where the watermelons grow,
Back to my home, I dare not go,
For if I do, my mother will say...
Did you ever have a time, when you couldn't make a rhyme,
Down by the bay?

29

Jamaica Farewell

Traditional

Down the way where the nights are gay, And the

sun shines bright-ly on the moun-tain-top,

I took a trip on a sail-ing ship, And when I

reached Ja - mai - ca I made a stop. But I'm

sad to say, I'm on my way,

Won't be back for man - y a day, My

heart is down, my head is turn-ing a-round, I

miss all my friends in Kings-ton town.

Down at the market you can hear,
All the ladies cry out while on their heads they bear,
Akie rice, salt fish are nice,
And the sun is fine any time of the year.

CHORUS

Sounds of laughter everywhere,
And the children sway to and fro,
I must declare that my heart is there,
Though I've been from Maine to Mexico.

CHORUS (twice)

31

Apples and Bananas

Traditional

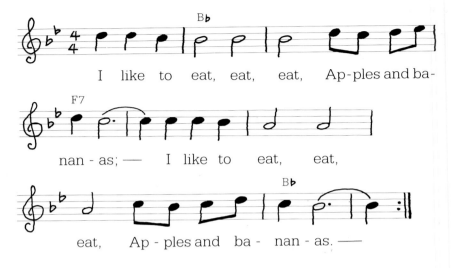

I like to eat, eat, eat, Ap-ples and ba-
nan - as; — I like to eat, eat,
eat, Ap - ples and ba - nan - as. —

I like to ate, ate, ate,
Ape-puls and ba-nay-nays;
I like to ate, ate, ate,
Ape-puls and ba-nay-nays;

I like to eat, eat, eat,
Ee-puls and bee-nee-nees;
I like to eat, eat, eat,
Ee-puls and bee-nee-nees;

I like to ite, ite, ite,
I-puls and bi-ni-nis;
I like to ite, ite, ite,
I-puls and bi-ni-nis;

I like to oat, oat, oat,
O-puls and bo-no-nos;
I like to oat, oat, oat,
O-puls and bo-no-nos;

I like to oot, oot, oot,
Oo-puls and boo-noo-noos;
I like to oot, oot, oot,
Oo-puls and boo-noo-noos;

Repeat first verse.

Chicken Lips and Lizard Hips

Cody Cassidy

Oh Chick-en lips and liz-ard hips and al- li- ga— tor eyes—

—— Mon-key legs and buz-zard eggs and sal— a- man-der

thighs Rab-bit ears and cam-el rears and tast-y toe- nail

pies Stir them all— to- geth— er, it's Ma-ma's Soup Sur-prise.

Oh, when I was a little kid I never liked to eat,
Mama'd put things on my plate, I'd dump them on her feet,
But then one day she made this soup, I ate it all in bed,
I asked her what she put in it, and this is what she said.

CHORUS

I went into the bathroom and stood beside the sink,
I said I'm feeling slightly ill, I think I'd like a drink,
Mama said "I've just the thing, I'll get it in a wink,
It's full of lots of protein, and vitamins I think."

CHORUS

Words and music by John and Nancy Cassidy © 1986 Klutz Press.

MAKE YOUR OWN

Comb Kazoo

Materials: Comb, tissue paper and stapler.

Instructions: Cut and staple a little square of tissue paper as shown so that you can slip the comb inside. Then hum through the comb and paper. To change pitch, just slide up and down like a harmonica.

Polly Wolly Doodle

Traditional

Oh, I went down South for to see my gal, Sing

pol - ly wol - ly doo - dle all the day, My —

Sal - ly is a spun - ky gal, Sing

pol - ly wol - ly doo - dle all the day. Fare thee

well, Fare thee well, Fare thee

well, my fair - y fay, For I'm

going' to Loui - si - an - a, For to

see my Su - zy - an - na, Sing

pol - ly wol - ly doo - dle all the day.

36

Oh, a grasshopper sittin' on a railroad track,
Sing polly-wolly-doodle all the day,
A-pickin' his teeth with a carpet tack,
Sing polly-wolly-doodle all the day.

CHORUS

Oh, I went to bed, but it wasn't no use,
Sing polly-wolly-doodle all the day,
My feet stuck out like a chicken roost,
Sing polly-wolly-doodle all the day.

CHORUS

This Old Man

Traditional

This old man, he played one, He played nick-nack

on my thumb, With a nick-nack pad-dy-wack,

Give the dog a bone, This old man came rolling home.

This old man, he played two,
He played nick-nack on my shoe,
With a nick-nack-paddy-wack,
Give the dog a bone,
This old man came rolling home.

This old man, he played three,
He played nick-nack on my knee,
With a nick-nack-paddy-wack,
Give the dog a bone,
This old man came rolling home.

This old man, he played four,
He played nick-nack on my door,
With a nick-nack-paddy-wack,
Give the dog a bone,
This old man came rolling home.

This old man, he played five,
He played nick-nack on my hive,
With a nick-nack-paddy-wack,
Give the dog a bone,
This old man came rolling home.

This old man, he played six,
He played nick-nack on my sticks,
With a nick-nack-paddy-wack,
Give the dog a bone,
This old man came rolling home.

This old man, he played seven,
He played nick-nack in my heaven,
With a nick-nack-paddy-wack,
Give the dog a bone,
This old man came rolling home.

This old man, he played eight,
He played nick-nack on my gate,
With a nick-nack-paddy-wack,
Give the dog a bone,
This old man came rolling home.

This old man, he played nine,
He played nick-nack on my spine,
With a nick-nack-paddy-wack,
Give the dog a bone,
This old man came rolling home.

This old man, he played ten,
He played nick-nack once again,
With a nick-nack-paddy-wack,
Give the dog a bone,
This old man came rolling home.

The Fox

Traditional

Oh the fox went out on a
chil - ly night, Prayed for the moon to
give him light, He'd man - y a mile to
go that night, Be - fore he reached the
town- o, town-o, town- o, He'd a
man - y a mile to go that night, Be -
fore he reached the town- o.

He ran until he came to a great big bin,
The ducks and the geese were put therein,
Said a couple of you are going to grease my chin,
Before I leave this town-o, town-o, town-o,
He said a couple of you are going to grease my chin,
Before I leave this town-o.

He grabbed the grey goose by the neck,
Slung the little one over his back,
He didn't mind their quack quack quack,
And the legs all dangling down-o, down-o, down-o,
No he didn't mind their quack quack quack,
And the legs all dangling down-o.

Old mother pitter patter jumped out of bed,
Out of the window she cocked her head,
Crying "John, John the grey goose is gone,
And the fox is on the town-o, town-o, town-o,"
Crying "John, John the grey goose is gone,
And the fox is on the town-o."

John he went to the top of the hill,
Blew his horn both loud and shrill,
The fox he said "I better flee with my kill,
For he'll soon be on my trail-o, trail-o, trail-o,"
The fox he said "I better flee with my kill,
For he'll soon be on my trail-o."

He ran 'til he came to his cozy den,
There were little ones, eight, nine, ten,
They said, "Daddy, Daddy, you better go back again,
For it must be a mighty fine town-o, town-o, town-o."
They said, "Daddy, Daddy, you better go back again,
For it must be a mighty fine town-o."

Then the fox and his wife without any strife,
Cut up the grey goose with a fork and a knife,
They never had such a supper in their life,
And the little ones chewed on the bones-o, bones-o, bones-o,
They never had such a supper in their life,
And the little ones chewed on the bones-o.

41

Twinkle, Twinkle Little Star

Traditional

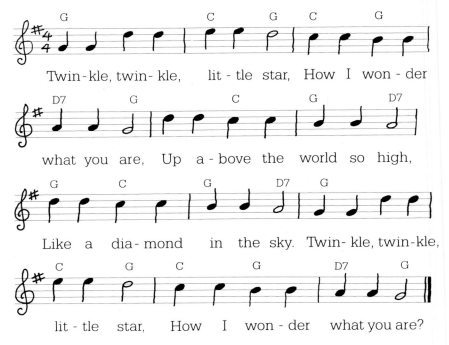

Twin-kle, twin-kle, lit-tle star, How I won-der what you are, Up a-bove the world so high, Like a dia-mond in the sky. Twin-kle, twin-kle, lit-tle star, How I won-der what you are?

When I go to sleep at night,
Thanks for keeping me in sight,
Please keep watch upon the earth,
Keep it safe 'til morning light.

Twinkle, twinkle, little star,
How I wonder what you are?

Puff (The Magic Dragon)

Leonard Lipton and Peter Yarrow

Together they would travel on a boat with billowed sail,
Jackie kept a lookout perched on Puff's gigantic tail,
Noble kings and princes would bow whene'er they came,
Pirate ships would low'r their flag when Puff roared out
   his name.

   CHORUS

A dragon lives forever but not so little boys,
Painted wings and giant rings make way for other toys,
One grey night it happened, Jackie Paper came no more,
And Puff that mighty dragon, he ceased his fearless roar.

His head was bent in sorrow, green scales fell like rain,
Puff no longer went to play along the cherry lane,
Without his lifelong friend, Puff could not be brave,
So Puff that mighty dragon sadly slipped into his cave.

   CHORUS

45

Morningtown Ride

Malvina Reynolds

Train whis-tle blow-ing, makes a sleep-y noise,

Un-der-neath their blan-kets, go all the girls and boys,

Head-ing from the sta-tion, out a-long the bay,

All bound for Morn-ing-town, man-y miles a-way.

Sarah's at the engine, Tony rings the bell,
John swings the lantern, to show that all is well,
Rocking, rolling, riding, out along the bay,
All bound for Morningtown, many miles away.

Maybe it is raining, where our train will ride,
But all the little travelers are snug and warm inside,
Somewhere there is sunshine, somewhere there is day,
Somewhere there is Morningtown, many miles away.

This Little Light of Mine

Traditional

This lit - tle light of mine, I'm gon-na let it shine,

This lit - tle light of mine, I'm gon-na let it shine,

This lit - tle light of mine, I'm gon-na let it shine, Let it

shine, let it shine, let it shine.

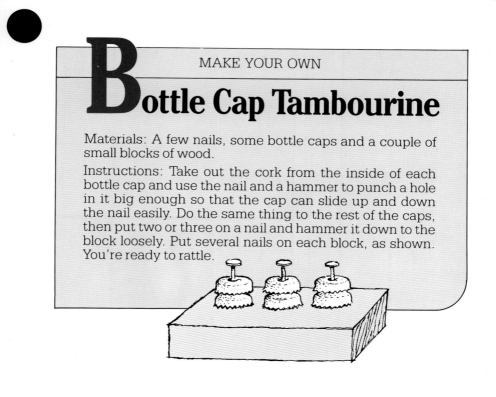

MAKE YOUR OWN

Bottle Cap Tambourine

Materials: A few nails, some bottle caps and a couple of small blocks of wood.

Instructions: Take out the cork from the inside of each bottle cap and use the nail and a hammer to punch a hole in it big enough so that the cap can slide up and down the nail easily. Do the same thing to the rest of the caps, then put two or three on a nail and hammer it down to the block loosely. Put several nails on each block, as shown. You're ready to rattle.

My brothers and my sisters, I'm gonna help them shine,
My brothers and my sisters, I'm gonna help them shine,
My brothers and my sisters, I'm gonna help them shine,
Help 'em shine, help 'em shine, help 'em shine.

This little love of ours, I'm gonna let it shine,
This little love of ours, I'm gonna let it shine,
This little love of ours, I'm gonna let it shine,
Let it shine, let it shine, let it shine.

This big world of ours, I'm gonna help it shine,
This big world of ours, I'm gonna help it shine,
This big world of ours, I'm gonna help it shine,
Help it shine, help it shine, help it shine.

The Kids Songs cassette was recorded by Nancy Cassidy in May, 1986, in Toronto, Ontario at the Wellesley Sound Studios and at Casa Rossmore. It was produced by Ken Whiteley and engineered by Roger Slemin.

Appearing on the cassette are:

Nancy Cassidy—lead vocals, guitar
Ken Whiteley—guitars (acoustic & electric), mandolin, synthesizer, piano, tambourine, jug, washboard, organ, accordion, washtub bass, triangle, high string guitar, banjo, autoharp, dobro, tenor banjo, kazoo, harmonica, rub board, slide guitar, mouth horn, Hawaiian guitar, train whistle.
Dennis Pendrith—electric bass
Bucky Berger—drums
Tom Szczesniak—accordion
Dave Piltch—string bass
Chris Whiteley—harmonica, trumpet
Grit Laskin—whistles, Appalachian dulcimer, concertina
Graham Townsend—fiddles
Dick Smith—conga, triangle, clave, pods, wood blocks
Earl Lapierre—steel drums
Ron Dann—pedal steel guitar
Jody Golick—soprano saxophone
Mose Scarlett—guitar, mouth horn
Caitlin Hanford—mouth horn
Scott Irvine—tuba
Sean Snell—cymbals

The Kids Choir:

Cindy Tse, Valerie Shaughnessy, Priya Glassey, Jamie Chiarelli, Mark & Damian Gryski, Toby Novogrodsky, Erin Bentley, Andrew Fussner, Eden Fussner, Ben Panton, Zoe Campbell, Matty Chavel, Angus McClaren.

Nancy Cassidy, the lead singer of Kids Songs, has been singing and writing music all of her life.

Ken Whiteley, the producer of Kids Songs, has arranged, produced, or performed on, much of the most creative and popular children's music of the past 10 years.